Under the Music of Blue

Dede Wilson

FUTURECYCLE PRESS
www.futurecycle.org

Library of Congress Control Number: 2017935334

Published by FutureCycle Press
Athens, Georgia, USA

ISBN 978-1-942371-26-7

For my granddaughters:
Waverly, Whitney and Westerly

Contents

I

To Wake.. 11

Morning.. 12

The Girl Who Danced on Her Hands by the Sea..................13

White... 14

If There Were the Sound of Water Only............................ 16

Still Morning.. 18

Seasons... 19

Seeing Her Grandfather Weep.. 20

A Day's Failed Silence... 21

Trying to Sleep in the Butterfly Room..............................22

Sleeplessness and the Absence of Rain............................. 23

Brush of a Dark Wing... 24

Perpetual Light in Marsh Grass...................................... 25

Three Green Pears in a Blue Pottery Bowl........................ 26

To Sleep.. 27

II

Dissonance of Dust on This Old Sunrise Photo: A Triptych..............31

Weaves: The Art of Abstraction in a Visible World..........................32

Love, That Gypsy Child, Knows No Laws...........................34

The Sun Rides on Its Own Melting....................................35

If They Should Clone Me.. 36

Judgment... 37

The Middle Tyger River... 38

To the Son Who Pasted His Ceiling in Stars.......................39

Barter... 40

Study of Her Mother.. 41

Scarecrow.. 42

Assassin on My Street... 43

Voice of the Wreckage... 44

Gathering Fears.. 45

Chameleon... 46

Seasons When Your Feet Can't Touch the Bottom..............47

To the Poets Writing of Wings.. 48
Old Motifs... 49
The Blue Silk Lounging Pajamas...50
City Pool... 52
Youth.. 53
Jewelry Store..54
When Mama Smiled...55
Line of Thought..56

III

I Speak to My Son of Old Excesses.. 59
Happy Hours.. 60
A World Begins to Speak.. 62
Feckless Rueing... 63
Tintinnabulations, or How to Live with Tinnitus............................64
Breaking Old Silences.. 65
Pulling the Last Word from under the Pillow................................ 66
Entering the Scholar's Room... 67
The Chinese Master's Brush... 68
Rustle of Praise.. 69
The Power Company.. 70
While I Sauté Apples and Onions to Stuff the Pork..........................71
Man in the Rain..72
To the Friend Whose Home Was Destroyed by Lightning................74
For Solomon, the New Parrot.. 75
The Sum of Many Summers..76
Birds Have Flown From My Hands.. 77
Ode to the Saguaro..78
The Time of My Dreams... 79
Man in the Lamplight with Lemons...80
I Drift in Darkness, Always Facing the Day..................................81
Unwrapping the Mummy.. 82
Leaving the Vineyard... 83
Longing for the Pleiades...84

The Ecstatic Man

—Ernst Barlach, small bronze figure

See how he covers his ears
with his forearms, fists bound
in his hair, and here is his brow,
lifted for more, and here
are his lips, for pain. Perhaps
it is you, Basho,
long strides, summer rain
weighting your mended britches,
your lug of rags and sack,
the winter sleet like switches
of willow whipping your back.
Though when the flawless word
breaks in your breast like a cord,
you, like anyone, fill
you, like anyone, shout
while the wind's skirl
and the flint of the road
drown you out.

1

To Wake

out of the shawl of darkness
  out of the collar of grief

out of the revenant-threaded dream
  pulse ticking against the sheets

the child under a halo of pain
  heartleaf fragrant in her hand

out of the night of the hummingbird moth
  caught in a moonflower's throat

oh to wake

  to branch and birdsong
the measure of bells

Morning

—*after Li Po*

Go.
    Make as little noise as you can.
        Night is rising out of your arms.
Day, alas, is no keeper of dreams.

The Girl Who Danced
on Her Hands by the Sea

      now runs
through dunes of wind and sound,
the salty breath
of the sonorous beast.

The wan sky she runs on
is a scintillate shim of sand,
a watered glaze, crazed
by wading birds.

Dawn in a haze rides the horizon.

      Sun strikes
a lone cloud. Hot white sparks
bore her eye, bare the day. Again

light hides, rising behind
a sum of exhalations,

while on and on
the vastness reels, the beat
of her feet, the sand at her heels,
the roll of the sea, *greedy,*
steamy, myth-riddled sea
her pulse repeats, deceived
by grief, residual and deep.

Just for a breath the water sleeps.

White

You are the soap-sound
    when I am singing
in showers

clock face
    day moon
pockets pulled out

(if I say
    like being awakened by mourning doves
you tend to gray)

you
    are truth
confessing

sharp
    as the edges of pages
a shatter of stars

bright
    as the shy child
baptized in daylight

you
    are the tongue
alight on a salt lick

the swan whose waxy feather
    will not fit
back in the ragged egg

milk
    glass unstained
underthings unpinned in rain

every color
    washed
out of being

you are the field
    where linen lay bleaching
in lye and buttermilk

the day
    paper
became you

enter
    any water
you will be bare

light as a kite
    string
lean

you are the loss of ivory
    afterlife
the speed of light

old bones
    raptured
in ice

If There Were the Sound of Water Only

—T. S. Eliot

When I walk into a room
   someone has just walked out of
broken an orange in

breathe in
   (breath) (zest)
fill

with (someone)
   (orange)
the need to ask

how much is all
   how much
makes anything whole

this necklace
   of her woven hair
or this

one open eye
   a locket
so painted

it becomes her
   all
I can do is ask

whose god is all
   whose god
makes anything whole

perhaps
   the god called Christ
whose bones

(claim villagers
   in Japan)
lie buried

under a simple mound
   in a town
called Shingo

where god-bells toll
   and palms fold
fists of smoke

where those denying
   afterlives
confide a fear of ghosts

whose god is all
   whose
god

fashioned the daughter
   who longed
to be flung to the sea

so we took her
   lonely comb to the shore
and there

released
   the (tea breeze) (sea breeze)
scent of her hair

Still Morning

From the horizon
        you are the horizon

lie cut by the sea as it curls
        under your feet

the cold sand
        the cumulus spume

moon floating
        broken and whole

any horizon
        is more than a penciled line

a draw of desire
        and discard

the *cry*
        cry

of the gull
        ease of a dive

into history
        and ruin

Seasons

Old sweaters, limp with the lost
inhalations of winter. Great
is the weight of all I am folding.

Call them! Call the children!
Gone their voices, high, high
as fiddler winds
strumming sharp new grasses.

(I cut the clay, planted iris
where she'd played.)

Each day
a child has a new face.
It fits like a name.

Come and let me tell you
how she came, unwilling
and afraid,
a bulb forced for a season.

She was born when I touched
my fingers
to the tips of her tiny ones.

We let her cry, that is the pain of it,
something we'd read somewhere.

Seeing Her Grandfather Weep

The craftsman says
    our heritage chestnut
        is a risk to cut.
Often a tree has fleshed around steel—

a horseshoe, blade or nail—abraded within,
    and contact with a mill saw
        will shatter
the heart of such aged wood.

A Day's Failed Silence

Rustle in the leaves.
    Rustle of God, I think.
        I sit on a bench, waiting.
Great seed pod crashes down.

One leaf settles, two leaves turn.
    Nothing of God, nothing
        but this pesky yellow honeybee
hymning around my knees.

Trying to Sleep
in the Butterfly Room

You will have everything
    if you settle for less
        mending the shredded tissue
of each day

sleep sleep lift
    your hand from the pillow
        self is all you want
to lose

wrapped and
    wingless body
        curtains blowing
folding

Sleeplessness and
the Absence of Rain

If there were clouds you'd hear the clouds
the way you're listening, straining
to every sound, the rumble
of jets, acorns splashing
your deck, and on your roof
the small parched feet of the creature
who scrubbed for moisture
under a wither of ferns, then ran
away from the absence
of rain—rain you know
you are hearing, that distant spitting
of trains, wind scraping the leaves,
the owl with his wide-eyed thirst,
the sough and hush of his call.

Brush of a Dark Wing

Dream, dream, sing your meaning to me.
I hold the pieces. Sleep keeps the whole.
While I drift through dusk to the green,
    night's still lowing *oh oh-old*.

I hold the pieces. Sleep keeps the whole.
So why this deep unease on waking, night
receding, dawn still lowing *oh oh-old*—
    the brush of a dark wing.

While I keep this deep unease, waking
out of the night, dream is leaving
the brush of a dark wing
    on the mirror of my eye.

Out of the night, the dream, leaving
the intricate weave of my sleep,
the mirror of my eye,
    I creep to the edge of the clearing.

Far from the intricate weave of sleep,
far from the dusk and into the green,
I plead from the clearing: dream,
    dream, sing your meaning to me.

Perpetual Light in Marsh Grass

When the herons break, they flame
against a stained-glass sky,

their legs like brittle wicks,
their wings on fire.

One heron like a candlestick
lights upon a pier. And yellow moths

and dragonflies leave sparks
as they fly by. In this cathedral's

umber dusk, when
fickle wind's full-swing,

it sings through beak and creekbone,
strums the marshgrass strings.

Three Green Pears
in a Blue Pottery Bowl

Gentlemen,
a little bluer, please,
Liszt is whispering
to his court musicians.

Imagine a shallow bowl
with three green pears,
the clay-cold edge
blue against his mind.

My grandmother lifting
a blue enameled bowl
to catch the beat of rain.
The clarity of rainwater
she saved to wash her hair.

Rain falling on pears.

Liszt's long fingers
ringing the rim of the bowl.

Pears ripening
under the music of blue.

To Sleep

out of the ash and residue
    out of the penniless winds

out of the peaks keening into ravines
    the fissure of myth

out of the lily's fallalery
    dressed as the wings of a swan

the yellow gorse crushed by Goliath
    in the valley of Elah

oh to sleep

    one long night
rapt in moonlight

II

Dissonance of Dust on This Old Sunrise Photo: A Triptych

this spill of sky in sea
this burnished fire
still shimmers the clouds
in mingled motes
of talcum and lint
of pollen and spore
and sieves to me
still sweeps to me
crusts of the stones
old seacoast seeds
our shores exhaled
so I bury my face
through sky's rough breath
in freckled air the way I buried
in earth-stirred dust
deep in his pillow and pulled
the light of
him in in deep sweet draughts
one metallic day
of sweat and oil and slough
a camera caught

Weaves: The Art of Abstraction in a Visible World

—with a line from Li He

lithe willows
    lacing the wind

sweetgrass so tight
    baskets carry water

Les Demoiselles d'Avignon
    rearranging line and plane

Flemish bond
    Jacob's ladder

skaters alight on a lake
    crosshatching ice

intersections
    mapped by Mondrian

hail strafing
    a wrought iron gate

Copland's atonal notes
    unraveling the score

a page turned
    words threaded over

shadows of blinds
    throw bamboo patterns

long black hair
    scribbling his pillow

sweet lacing at dawn
    day's gates

Love, That Gypsy Child, Knows No Laws

any beginning
        of lust
or expectation

that touch
        of bare
astonishment

pale
        expectant belly
of the moon

sasanqua white
        as a pearl
unstrung

figs
        in the trees
heavy as tears

something gnawing
        again
in the walls

The Sun Rides on
Its Own Melting

For days now I've been grinding my nails.
The snail's moist head's caught in its shell.
Cicadas are winding, unwinding the pines.

I am sitting on splinters, dusts of shell and sand.
My wry glass on the rail. The parched lips of leaves.
This day a body too withered to hold.

Squirrels are chewing their tails, pine voles
choosing cool chambers. The cat on the sill,
fiddling with twigs, chill as a fossil in amber.

If They Should Clone Me

If they placed me in my arms
   how could I carry
the density

of the knowledge
   of me
more than twin

more than lamb
   leaving the meadow
of mother

trick of man
   who you are I am
I am

(I am imagining
   I would be twiced
there could be more of me)

     not me   not me

orphan
   of desire
I could not bear your innocence

     how could I
         console you?

Judgment

This is the poem my life built.
    Seasons of self. Seasons of play.
    All the good I cannot repay.
This is my faded rag-stitched quilt

of days I've lost: from days of milk
    to soon-forgotten yesterday.
    This is the poem my life built
through hours of waste and disarray.

Why do I labor under guilt,
    try to retract, revise, replay?
    Is memory life's cruel exposé?
I hide the threads of gilded silk
when I write the poem my life built.

The Middle Tyger River

—sign on I-85, rural South Carolina

Every time I drive this road,
I search for the first—*Tyger South?*
And watch for the last. But, no, I've sped on by,
my head still caught in the Middle Tyger's mouth.

Dazzling kingdom of conceit! This stream's
knee-deep. No burning eye or symmetry
to stalk my sleep. Exaggerated mystery
in one pretentious sign. Such shallow lies!

And what in his hunger is ever the same?
What must he bear behind his yellow eye?
And whether he stalks or simply presides,
what of wildness still paces his veins?

Of majesty—knowing where waters flow?
What of cunning—art and claw?

To the Son Who Pasted His Ceiling in Stars

—after Henri Rousseau, The Sleeping Gypsy

One dark note
   under a moon
      of borrowed light.
You lie dreaming

on the sand. I haunt
   the landscape,
      cannot lift you
from recumbent sleep, suffer

your wide-eyed waiting beast.
   Soon you'll wake
      to linear strands
of linen and hair,

mane and music.
   Your mandolin
      beside you.
Its open throat.

Barter

My brother says he would not give
a fig for my inclinations. Well,

I'd not trade my son's thick beard
for his son's jeweled ear.

Husband, would you be me
in this art of unbinding my feet?

I know I'd take your childlike sleep
in exchange for my intuitions.

I'd even swap my midnight hours
for your hours of dawn, the sun

wide and rising. But I'd not choose
to barter loss for loss.

Study of Her Mother

—for W. L. H.

Slim fingers.
    Slender smokes.
        Dark hair
inked to her head.

Empire table.
    Tang bowl with potpourri.
        One martini,
spear and pearly onion.

Telephone. Black
    as a schoolgirl's convent skirt.
        Long white teeth
when she speaks.

She wears nothing but black.
    Her rooms nothing but white.
        Arrangement in.
Birds at the window fly suddenly off.

Red blazing
    into the room.
        Schoolgirl, schoolgirl,
flashing a scarf.

But back to black and white.
    For this is where we are.
        Martini. Clove and sooty orange peel
in her potpourri.

Blur of the daughter—
    with a matchstick—
        charring her name
on each white wall.

Scarecrow

Blowsy wind has filled her sleeves,
her ribs, with rumors of flesh.

And her broomstick arms
no longer sweep a woman's curve.

It is only illusion
she waves

away dark birds, her head
a chatter of pie tins, her hands

a gather of straw. She does not
know her shadow

lying fallow on the field
is the cross she bears

upon those fleshy melons,
mouths full, cheeks flushed.

Assassin on My Street

You see the smoke
before you hear the crack
and whine of metal
speeding straight
through time so slowed
you know
you'll catch it in your hands
and stop this
slick of blood so wet so red
so now
you lay you down
between the sun-bleached sheets
she pinned along the line
you danced beneath in summer
air you still can breathe
since you're still breathing
in this trick of time
that's whistling
like a bullet through your bone

Voice of the Wreckage

     Circle
my smoldering bones,
wrist-hinge and shin. Shine
your false light, searching
for what I am not.
     And when you stagger
upon my lone gold ring, you will
be wedded to absence. I am
a tissue-thin stain
to add to the earth's striata:
bloodfall, breastmilk, body
of little but water, rich vein
of memory you are measuring.

     So I will tell you:
one sharp breath was all we took away.

Now my sigh, gauze lung in the leaves,
feeds your zeal for flame. And when
the last smoke lifts, filled
with flesh, I leave you
     hungered.

Gathering Fears

I fill my pockets with nails
 someone has tossed in the street
to ruin our tires, to wound our feet.

Who knows what evil prevails.
 Home, I fling out my pockets.
My pockets are filled with sticks.

Chameleon

He flushes green to cling to mint
   or molds to rock in sullen umber
     as though a crayoned ghost,
for even the hint of ghost

must stay concealed. Perhaps
   most ghosts, caught in the blush
     of dying, turn aubergine
and nest among the plums.

For what is a ghost
   but the stain of memory?
     Here we speak
of other ways of hiding, behind

the curtain of prayers
   where we beg for our children's lives
     so long it is superstition:
Our Father, who art in inner space,

spare me the wraiths
   of your wretched garden.
     Make me chameleon.
Hide me.

Seasons When Your Feet
Can't Touch the Bottom

Though truth will briefly light
upon the surface, little I see

is clear or predictable. My eyes
are level with the glare, and water

gnats annoy my brows. I am
no more than water snake—

quick eye, quick line, divining.
Colder and colder my lonely pond

till I am clasped in ice.
I wait and wait for the thaw,

the break of wet lilies
wild for the light.

To the Poets
Writing of Wings

How can muse be piqued to quiddle with quills?
Backs are lustrous to the touch, skin unruffled,

yet you speak of *feathers, molt, preen,*
as though with wings we'd live

the easeful lives of dragonflies,
as though we'd drift along, feeding

on the wind. No more
batting tattered rings around

some fusty core. I mock
your feathers, dragging dust, your blades

that ache to flutter and soar, would *beg*
for wings if wings would lift us.

Old Motifs

I'll take what comes and humming hurry home.
Life is known for its upending ways.
If you are gone, and time and I alone

trace patterns on the wall repeating old
motifs—die and weep—indeed I'll rage,
then take what comes and humming hurry home.

I'll never fall to bed with teas and moans
or lamely swallow what my doctor names.
If you are gone, time and I alone

will tie our wilted stems to stiff-back stakes.
Never ready, claims the sage,
to take what comes and humming hurry home.

Day by day the shadowed psalm's intoned.
I'm still a little girl, said Mama, dazed,
her sisters gone. Time and she alone

living yet—last of seven, laced,
beloved and petted in the days of grace.
But all were gone, and time and she alone
took what comes and humming hurried home.

The Blue Silk
Lounging Pajamas

This was her story: the winding
stair he climbed to carry
her up to her room
after he'd found her, flung over
the grand piano, tipsy and weeping.
He was there for a date with her sister.
She'd been waiting for Johnny.
But as my father lifted her
in those silk pajamas
under that dome of stars,
she wept on, holding close
the no-show telegram from Johnny.

Our mother told and told this,
proving she never cared
to forget it. Finally she showed us
her tissue-wrapped treasure.

But when she was old, ill,
and we swept her closets,
emptied her pockets and boxes
of any and all desires,
we found the silk pajamas
had disappeared.

From her sick bed Mama confessed:
I gave them to Leah.

We beseeched
the maid (I bribed, I cried),
who said that they had been sent
in a sack to her country sisters.

And the blue pajamas
with tarnished wings on the sleeves—
birds of beads and silver—
grew dearer and dearer,
being lost.

City Pool

I wore the suit of yellow wool
  that gripped my lean slick body

like a rind. In the sun
  it steamed its wet-fur stench, itched

and tightened out of water, coiled
  in my crotch like a rope.

I sat on the side,
  pulling and scratching, chewing

the whips of my wet hair,
  eyes on the high dive, back

to her painted nails
  laced in the chain links, Mama's face

waiting for me
  to slip in the deep, to live.

Youth

Though speeding
away from the past,
you won't forget
the day you drove
around, around
the empty field
with the top down,
stirring a cloud
of dust so high
the sun shone through,
gilt-edged,
and you so young
this could go on
and on, the tilt
of the car, the way
you soared
into and over
the dust to find
that clear sky
you were made of.

Jewelry Store

Our mother sent us
as soon as we could drive.
A way to help,
pick up a gift, wait
for its wrapping.
I can see me
standing there
in my brightness,
a scrubbed glass case
filled with every gift
a town could use.
I liked to banter
with Mr. Field.

He gave each girl
a silver spoon
the day she graduated.

Mr. Field is dead now.
So is my daughter.
I try to imagine me dead.
I mean in that unpolished time,
like someone smashing
all of those cases,
breaking treasures
while they're still new.

When Mama Smiled

She bit into the tender core of you.
Lips so crimped, a hairpin from her hair
must have come undone and fastened there.

None of us escaped her excavations,
forehead terse, mouth a trenchant line.
Oh merriment, come crack our mama's spine!

If she laughed, you had to catch it quick.
A glimpse of teeth, one small caught breath,
then all would disappear without a sound.

And we'd forget. Or wonder, did we hear
that jangled key, that unintended note?
Silences we found too true to bear.

Line of Thought

Design
    cannot fulfill its perfect line.
        A line electric dazzles as it breaks.
Sunline fractures into shadow.

Draw your gaze along the far horizon—
    peaks and steeples break in line.
        Even rain when plumb
takes the shape of all it falls upon.

If I stand before you, tall
    on stilts of slim bamboo,
        I cannot mimic
Roman numeral II—

the line, to balance, bends.
    And strings laid straight
        along the lute
must wend to sing.

We are taught
    that any line
        between two points
deceives

and arcs.
    Like the smile Mona Lisa's
        moving smoothly into.
Or out of.

III

I Speak to My Son
of Old Excesses

I want you there,
a child in my childhood,
stuffed with three meats, two
kinds of potatoes, sipping
from goblets with dollops of wine—
even for children. Here, savor
the uncles who teased us
at table, talked over
our heads. We ate and ate, more
than our bodies could carry, stumbled
out to the porch, swimmy
in ears, swaying like honeysuckle
weighted with bees.

Happy Hours

and what would Fran have done
without her glass
her little napkin
of impeccable linen
twisted in her hand
we loved this beautiful aunt's

angle of elbow
firm against her wheelchair's steel
she was daring fate
drinking with MS
but who's to say
it didn't get her through

and my father
who poured with a heavy hand
tipped the decanter
for nips of sherry after church
and when I ripened
into a woman's complaints

he placed a silver spoon
in a crystal glass
shook in sugar
a jigger of bourbon
tilted the kettle and offered a toddy
hot to soothe and confuse

oh so good to feel it
nothing like the vanilla extract
I drank in the pantry with my best friend
waiting
all one afternoon
for something to change

the aunts in the Delta are well-preserved
they sit on open porches playing rubbers of bridge
if it's not five
someone turns the clock
glasses of bourbon sweat in the heat
maids bring chocolates and ice

my mother's the life of the party
two or three sips and she's on
the night she was jilted and got in her papa's bourbon
(she tells this story on herself
how she was wearing silk pajamas
blue with lush embroidery)

she swooned
over the piano in her parents' parlor
and the man she would marry
scooped her into his arms and carried her
up the winding staircase
dizzy for good

and I was born
out of the liquid bodies
into the arguable joy
I was born
little sweetener
and everyone raised a glass

A World Begins
to Speak

First the dark,
a stutter of stars.
Stones sloped like tongues.

Where are the hollows for mouths?
And who the uninhibited digger
boring into dust?

Simply the sea, indecisive, wanting,
not wanting the shore?

Moon, that cold opal, opens throats to Os.

So
    cheeks go swollen, overflowing
with sound.

A scribble of teeth.
    A hieroglyph.

I. Aye. Fire.

Now *argument.*

Feckless Rueing

Our mother is telling us, over and over,
what she has lost, her brothers and sisters
tumbling down the stairs, breaking
every bone of their past.
She seems to insist the ceiling
was made of stars. One by one,
she says, the pasted papers peeled away.
We can feel the paper cuts
slip beneath our skins.
We let her sorrows in.

Tintinnabulations, or
How to Live with Tinnitus

You can listen but you can't hear
the ringing sounds that fill my ears

with after-hymns of chapel bells,
the sighs of tides in empty shells.

Shrieks of silences escaping veils.
The screel of icy crevices unsealed.

Hums of the ones who rub their wings.
A chill of chainsaws—lingering.

Secrets the kettle is begging to spill.
Apples singing as they're peeled.

Breaking Old Silences

The sky, a camouflage
   of clouds. Snow
unfolds its sheets.

The children, fallen
   angels,
carving wings

like silver teaspoons
   breaking crusted sugar.
Boots emboss the snow.

On lips a taste
   of moon, sliver
of ice in cream.

The crow
   on ravaged wings
weaves through

spits of sleet.
   Wounds moan
in the throat of the wind.

Pulling the Last Word
from under the Pillow

No getting away from it, this breaking
    into fragments
        that fall on the bedclothes,
on Eros, on pesky Id,

that become the oblivious dust
    on the table beside the bed,
        eye-level,
like an accusation.

In the brutal light
    I run my finger over surfaces.
        Galaxies shimmer, dance,
succumb and fall.

I lie still
    in my mere infinity.
        It does not matter
that so little of dust is dust.

Entering the Scholar's Room

—Philadelphia Museum of Art

All the brushes have handles of jade

He touches his scroll
　　his hands
like spiders straddling grasses

In washes of lacquer and bone dust
　　he paints
a bowl of blue plums

Moon is his inkstone

He knows how my sister
　　is combing the lawn
dragging her basket of grass

He knows how my mother
　　is drawing her mouth
up out of sorrow

He knows how the rock in the cradle whines

(Now I am quivering
　　like paper and lips
humming a tortoise-shell comb)

He knows how my father lifted me
　　high
above his head

He knows
　　how I lifted the glasses
from my father's face

He knows how I break at the knees

The Chinese Master's Brush

A sweep of prunus blossoms on the snow—
his wrist is quick, depicts a branch. A trick,

it seems, the bough alive in one sure flick.
I try my hand. A stuttered flow.

Color into color weeps,
my stroke unsteady, wavy as a flame.

Yet I'll still trust I'd earn the master's name
if he'd bequeath his mythic brush to me.

I'll paint the slickest eggplant, plum or grape,
the sagest cock to strut across a page.

Rustle of Praise

the living seed   sweet core of a pear
    moon in the cherries
sun polishing the plums

winter's scribble of twigs
    spring and its rustle of praise
birds in the leaves   a silky fleet of wings

coffee   cinnamon   lemons   pecans
    the tree that feeds
the harmony of groves

shade   paths through patches of gladness
    burl   the wound concealed
the scars and eccentricities of rings

willow   maple   hemlock   oak and elm   pine
    the axe that fells   the match that burns
our grieving choirs of trees

The Power Company

Five men
are felling the pines.

I am told
not to be sentimental.
I am told the sky will mend
and the pine-snagged moon
will soon drift free.

My breath is sharp with resin.
The sun is sticky and whole.

In my slippers in wet grass
I stand and listen
to chew-sounds of chainsaws
that vibrate like locusts
devouring everything green.

*

Beside the curb on Third,
the street they should call Main,
Mama's car is idling,
waiting for me to climb in.
I flee the salon, open the door, fall
to the back seat's wool, sheared
and weeping. "It will grow back,"
she says, "before you know it."

*

Morning moves from leaf to leaf.
My trees fill with bright orange men.

While I Sauté Apples and Onions to Stuff the Pork

I count the meals I've made. The years.
The steps. The trips. The falls.
Don't count the tears. Count
the change. The penny we leave
on the street. The cash we keep.
Those who have shared the feasts. Who've watched
them baste the suckling pig strung from a tree.
Lifted the pitcher for countless gulps of tea.
Who could count the babies laid on quilts
to change? I have changed. I'm not who I think I am.
And why do I count if you count the numbers of souls.
The ones who are leaving. The ones who are left.
God knows, so many souls. Let's see...
I think this needs a bit of thyme, a trace of sage.

Man in the Rain

I kind of fancy my suit,
    if you don't mind,
        he says as he stuffs
his coat, his pants, his shoes

into a garbage bag
    the waiter has brought
        to the table, lifts
the plastic package

high above his head
    and—leaving
        those fluted oysters
whole in their shells—

wades out of Arnaud's
    through waters so smarmy
        they're turning sludge
and excrements

to ripe stains on his shins
    while rain keeps
        raining
over the open awning

of the Napoleon House
    where we're listening
        to music
flowing

out of the old Victrola
    and draining
        tumblers of gin
while pouring

out of the spouts
    of our mouths
        stories of rain,
the man in the rain,

smiling, waving—
    don't you remember
        how he'd insisted
that *yes, oh yes,*

the day would come
    when water would run through the streets
        and swallow the houses, swelling
the wicker, logging the walls—

and we would laugh,
    oh how we'd laugh,
        raising our glasses,
toasting the rain.

To the Friend Whose Home Was Destroyed by Lightning

After that flash, that bolt
from bed—warm bed, the book

beside her closed and marked
just hours before—and through

the nearest door to rain
pasting her gown like paper

to her skin, does it matter
what she's lost

when she's lost all?
She doesn't own a spoon.

Women in our town
keep trying on her cloth of loss,

even wondering
how it feels to be released

from all we hold and keep
and what keeps us.

For Solomon, the New Parrot

Here at the inn with a view of the sea,
    we drink the sun in our cups while old
summers fade from the cage.

Speak to me, Solomon. Sweet. *Sweet!*
    Dew feeds the fig bush.
Morning is damp on the chairs.

Green, green, this new parrot's green,
    pretty—and surely no vices.
Wind is pulling a darkness over our heads.

Ah, the leaf-smell of rain,
    pocked wet sand,
sounds in the shell a cochlea repeats.

Here by the lattice, the unlatched
    door of Solomon's cage,
talons grip my sleeve.

The Sum of
Many Summers

You no longer dance on the sand,
    or run, or spin,
        though you still plumb
the surf and lunge

through sea's salt breath, while here and there
    a lone ghost crab
        stilts and feints, then
scrams. You, my friend,

plug on and on, each step a bold
    intaglio
        the tide will soon
fill up, tip in.

Birds Have Flown From My Hands

So Little Jerry's dead.
  And Mama's breaking

the sky with a hammer
  like she's breaking ice.

Time will bend
  and scatter, pages fly,

I'll lay waste to days.
  Blinking the sand

from my eyes,
  I laugh. I rage.

Death has paged me twice.
  Such disruption!

At this age, I might give in,
  take it for flattery.

Ode to the Saguaro

Perhaps that fluttering in your flesh
is birds who've filled you with their nests.
They've riddled you with chiseling.

Cool and white, your summer blossoms
ripen dark and figgy. Few seeds survive.
The desert feasts. And winds lose some.

Beneath your folds a filigree
of lattices and ribs. Here sponges hold
life for those who thirst near you.

I'd never laugh at how you stand—arms in poses,
leg flamingoed in the sand. I understand.
I know how old you are, how old I am.

The Time of My Dreams

A day is a day, but it does press down.
Awake, you find the hour is chained
and you are chained to useless wings
beating your clouds of time to cream.
Make a list. You make a list
to fill the day. Days unfold. This,
or each thing you cross out—*done*—
sighs and fractures into ten.
The mail brings surveys and assignments.
Summer, so it must be ironed.
Time climbs up to press its visage,
unforgiveness, in your face.
Try again. Feet on the tile.
Juice, paper, bath, time
to button and unbutton, one by one.
The more you do, the more you get done,
you've heard that old cliché.
But the reverse? One task can fill a day?
Sure, your resting heartbeat's fast,
but are you really built to last
through pause and chime and wilt of hours,
through all your idleness devours?

Man in the Lamplight
with Lemons

He does not see
the bowl of lemons
under the lamp

as more than mere décor.
He lolls in his chair—
all *zzzz*, no zest. Dozes.

I'd kiss his dry lips,
the rinds of his cheeks
oily and bright,

but why would I
disturb a still life?
He does not see me

leap up, lob lemons.
He does not know
I've turned out the light.

I Drift in Darkness, Always Facing the Day

I tell you, I'm not afraid
for death to whirl me
through the cosmic nebulae I'll be
stunned to be, no need
for one great sun to appear
to drop below the pines
or rise behind
a shell's long shadow
on sand, for all I am
and all that burns
will hurl a steely light
like no light known
on slowly rolling earth.
Yet, *not yet, not yet,*
for in that haze of vaporous glare,
in that blaze of carnival fires,
would I not long for
one lone cloud, one shadow?

Unwrapping the Mummy

Peel the endless linen.
   Listen

to memories
   rattling like seed pods.

Trace the papery omega
   of breast and hands.

And when you pare your nails
   and toss the leavings,

and when you walk on the streets
   scattering hairs,

the stains on the sheets
   are lives you are washing

out of the cloth.
   We make so much of remains.

Leaving the Vineyard

A grape that hasn't suffered
will never give something good,
insists the vintner whose yields
go back two hundred years.
I've already learned it takes
dark grapes of *pinot noir*
to brace the best champagne,
that weeds between the rows
deepen vineyard roots.

Far from tender vineyards
where vines, sharply pruned,
weep with fruit, I tilt
my glass, turn the page.
A child, smiling in the sun,
appears between the lines,
spirals toward the margin.
I don't mind.
Grapes are rolling over
the sympathy of my tongue.
I'm pouring the years into wine.

Longing for the Pleiades

My grandmother's house. The high-domed hall.
All of the heavens papered in stars.
I counted Seven Sisters, knowing only five,
begged for the fallen moon. Soon
the paper night was light-washed white.

*

We played on the pier with pails of stars.
Nova, supernova, clouds of shimmering
gas and dust. I'd close my eyes.
Shattered light showed dark
where stars had glowed.

*

Under the mirrored ball we danced,
stars passing through us, stars
on all like silver kisses.

*

At the fair, paper birds
twirled overhead like quickened years—
sidereal years—to startle
into the black hole
that does not remember not to exist.

*

New York City. A whirlwind trip
to see Van Gogh. I rode the spirals,
slipped into the dizzied centers
of his spinning stars.

*

Injected with radioactive
isotopes, I watched
the galaxies of my heart
gather on a screen, not knowing
what they'd tell. We pulse
to a universe
where stars explode:
radiate, dim, return,
begin again.

*

The lamp beside my bed
tells me nothing. I lie still,
longing for the Pleiades.
If the stars have all gone out,
how long will they take
to let us know?

Acknowledgments

Grateful acknowledgment is made to the editors of the following journals in which these poems first appeared:

Asheville Poetry Review: "Voice of the Wreckage"
Atlanta Review: "While I Sauté Apples and Onions to Stuff the Pork"
California Quarterly: "Ode to the Saguaro" (as "Poem to the Saguaro on My 70th Birthday")
Carolina Quarterly: "Scarecrow"
Cave Wall: "Sleeplessness and the Absence of Rain"
Crucible: "A World Begins to Speak"
Hampden Sydney Poetry Review: "The Sun Rides on Its Own Melting"
Iodine: "Trying to Sleep in the Butterfly Room," "Man in the Lamplight with Lemons," "Leaving the Vineyard"
Kakalak: "White," "Man in the Rain," "The Sum of Many Summers," "Dissonance of Dust on this Old Sunrise Photo: A Triptych" (First Place Award, 2015)
Keystone Magazine: "Longing for the Pleiades" (First Place Award)
Main Street Rag: "Love, That Gypsy Child, Knows No Laws," "Brush of a Dark Wing"
New Mexico Poetry Review: "Study of Her Mother"
New Orleans Review: "Happy Hours"
One: "If There Were the Sound of Water Only"
Persimmon Tree: "Youth"
Plainsongs: "Breaking Old Silences"
Poem: "Old Motifs," "Jewelry Store," "For Solomon, the New Parrot"
South Carolina Poetry Review: "The Power Company"
Southern Poetry Review: "Line of Thought"
Spoon River Poetry Review: "The Time of My Dreams" (as "Retirement or the Time of Your Dreams")
Tampa Review: "To the Poets Writing of Wings"
Tar River Poetry: "Gathering Fears"
Wellspring: "City Pool," "Perpetual Light in Marsh Grass"

The following poems appear in anthologies: "Voice of the Wreckage" (*Asheville Poetry Review* 10th Anniversary Anthology) and "The Ecstatic Man" (*Southern Poetry Anthology: NC*).

"Morning" appeared on the blog of North Carolina Poet Laureate (2005-09) Kathryn Stripling Byer.

"Rustle of Praise," written on request for Arbor Day 2012, appears on the Charlotte Tree Advisory Committee's website as "Arbor Day."

Some of the poems in this collection were included in the following chapbooks: *Glass,* Scots Plaid Press (1998), one of two finalists in the Persephone Press Chapbook Competition; *Sea of Small Fears,* winner, 2001 Main Street Rag Chapbook Contest; and *Near Waking,* Finishing Line Press (2013).

Cover artwork, "All Blues," by Carolyn WarmSun; author photo by Ed Wilson; cover and interior book design by Diane Kistner; Georgia text and Aladin titling

About FutureCycle Press

FutureCycle Press is dedicated to publishing lasting English-language poetry books, chapbooks, and anthologies in both print-on-demand and Kindle ebook formats. Founded in 2007 by long-time independent editor/publishers and partners Diane Kistner and Robert S. King, the press incorporated as a nonprofit in 2012. A number of our editors are distinguished poets and writers in their own right, and we have been actively involved in the small press movement going back to the early seventies.

The FutureCycle Poetry Book Prize and honorarium is awarded annually for the best full-length volume of poetry we publish in a calendar year. Introduced in 2013, our Good Works projects are anthologies devoted to issues of universal significance, with all proceeds donated to a related worthy cause. Our Selected Poems series highlights contemporary poets with a substantial body of work to their credit; with this series we strive to resurrect work that has had limited distribution and is now out of print.

We are dedicated to giving all of the authors we publish the care their work deserves, making our catalog of titles the most diverse and distinguished it can be, and paying forward any earnings to fund more great books.

We've learned a few things about independent publishing over the years. We've also evolved a unique, resilient publishing model that allows us to focus mainly on vetting and preserving for posterity poetry collections of exceptional quality without becoming overwhelmed with bookkeeping and mailing, fundraising activities, or taxing editorial and production "bubbles." To find out more about what we are doing, come see us at www.futurecycle.org.

The FutureCycle Poetry Book Prize

All full-length volumes of poetry published by FutureCycle Press in a given calendar year are considered for the annual FutureCycle Poetry Book Prize. This allows us to consider each submission on its own merits, outside of the context of a contest. Too, the judges see the finished book, which will have benefitted from the beautiful book design and strong editorial gloss we are famous for.

The book ranked the best in judging is announced as the prize-winner in the subsequent year. There is no fixed monetary award; instead, the winning poet receives an honorarium of 20% of the total net royalties from all poetry books and chapbooks the press sold online in the year the winning book was published. The winner is also accorded the honor of being on the panel of judges for the next year's competition; all judges receive copies of all contending books to keep for their personal library.

www.ingramcontent.com/pod-product-compliance
Lightning Source LLC
Chambersburg PA
CBHW070006100426
42741CB00012B/3128